Advance praise

Everything Thaws by R

In EVERYTHING THAWS, bodies and memories break through the (supposed) permafrost. R. B. Lemberg's haunting poetic cycle is unsparing and keenly observed. Tracing their path from Ukraine to the Vorkuta GULAG, Hungary, Israel, and the USA, Lemberg crafts an unforgettable cartography of trauma, Jewishness, gender, war, and family history. This book expertly traverses dangerous ground. Children play in forests littered with bombs, and life-saving bridges disappear in snowstorms. In such terrain, a wrong step could mean death, yet there is no choice but to keep moving. Against cruelties, enforced silences, and the weight of generational horror, what can Lemberg do except "put it all into poems, / or, when the guilt gets too much, into turnips"? The thaw may be disastrous, but it must be faced, and Lemberg masterfully holds our gaze.

—**Izzy Wasserstein**, author, *All The Hometowns You Can't Stay Away From*

These are poems of reflection and empowerment, a journey of (self-) discovery brimming with raw feeling and a survivor's courage and wisdom. Lemberg excels at boldly drawing vivid scenes, memorable and complex characters, and emotionally charged landscapes. A deeply moving reading experience.

—**Vitaly Chernetsky**, author *Mapping Postcommunist Cultures: Russia and Ukraine in the Context of Globalization*

"Turn it and turn it, for every thing is in it": R.B. Lemberg's work has long been full of observations of the stark, the painful, and the utterly true. Taking its opening cue from the wreck of our climate, EVERYTHING THAWS is a swift-flowing personal history and a biting cultural commentary. It is also an intricate-illuminated map through what can't help emerging from that thaw: the diaspora of transness, Jewishness, how to be a parent, how to be a child. I was so stunned by its honesty and its hope; I have read and re-read it and there is always something newly revealed.

—**Jeannelle M. Ferreira**, author of *The Fire and the Place in the Forest*

R. B. Lemberg is "done destroying [themselves] for the sake of that anxiety of needing to look as if nothing ever happened." These poems are full of what happened — the food that was stolen to survive, the gender fails, the towns that no one believes existed, the near deaths and the gravesites. According to Lemberg, the past and the cold are as heavy and fragile as the thawing permafrost. While reading Everything Thaws, you'll feel the fleeting nature of everything we've named permanent, until "the truth itself is cratering."

—**Sass Orol**, author, *The Shortest Skirt in Shul*

Everything Thaws

A Poetic Cycle

R.B. Lemberg

Teaneck, New Jersey

Published by Ben Yehuda Press
122 Ayers Court #1B
Teaneck, NJ 07666

http://www.BenYehudaPress.com

To subscribe to our monthly book club and support independent Jewish publishing, visit https://www.patreon.com/BenYehudaPress

Jewish Poetry Project #26   **http://jpoetry.us**

Ben Yehuda Press books may be purchased at a discount by synagogues, book clubs, and other institutions buying in bulk. For information, please email markets@BenYehudaPress.com

ISBN13 978-1-953829-31-3

Library of Congress Cataloging-in-Publication Data

22 23 24 / 10 9 8 7 6 5 4 3 2 1   20230209

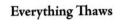

Everything Thaws

1.

Everything thaws. I learned this lately
when the permafrost in Vorkuta started to give way,
revealing secrets nobody asked for:
not wooly mammoths or ancient cave artifacts but
bodies of the GULAG prisoners thrown out — not even buried
because the snow would take care of its own.

You could trust the snow back then. And now you can't
trust anything.

Let me tell you why this matters to me.
When I was four, my father came into the room where I slept and kissed
me —

it was not "my" room. We only had two,
serving as gathering/art/working/sleep space as needed.
He thought I was asleep. I was.
My spirit hovered by the door, high by the twelve-foot ceiling
while I watched him lean over the slats of the bed.

He said nothing I could hear,
but he loved me, and he was leaving — that was clear,
leaving on the train and then on the train again,
three solid days of travel,
going north beyond the Arctic circle
to live for a while in Vorkuta
where once they killed people in the GULAG, but many
survived and either did not want or could not leave,

among them a distant relative of my mother's, who said he would help
my father to find a job and stay there
because the KGB was bothering him
here in Ukraine,
demanding he inform on his friends,
but he would not.

A few decades later
I began to write a story about this: the GULAG
to the west of the Ural Mountains, prisoners who flew around

as willow ptarmigans. "There was
no GULAG in Europe," a crit partner informed me
with the usual confidence of white Americans.
She was an expert, you see,
having researched GULAGs for her own story. She did not know
about Vorkutlag,
and so it did not exist.
She meant no harm, but she kept writing and I
stayed silent.

Long after we left Vorkuta, the melting permafrost
which I am witnessing over social media
disturbs me. Two continents and as many lifetimes ago
my father was happy there. Perhaps nobody else was, but he was,

far away from the KGB,
not so far away from my mother (but far enough),
snug in his wooden studio
assigned to him by the Soviet Artists' Union.
Among plates of colored glass, among
his glass-cutters and chisels and his blocks of wood,
the snow forever clenching the ground
its vast masses hiding all the dead; there he was
as permanent as permafrost, just as silent
but warmer.

I do not know how to mourn him in my five languages (nothing serves),
across three continents, with all my eloquence (nothing serves),
with all my silence (nothing serves)
for readers who might not believe
there ever was a Vorkuta, a circumpolar town where
thousands of GULAG prisoners died of malnutrition and exposure, where
architects plotted victory against permafrost, where
schoolchildren bullied other schoolchildren

by tying dead lemmings to strings and spinning them about.

When I came back to Ukraine
after a year in Vorkuta
I drew the northern lights to show my classmates. I drew myself
dragging a little sleigh, head up to the vast shimmering road in the sky.
It was my road

R. B. Lemberg

that showed me the way when I was six —
white, wide, stretching across the black winter sky
in complete silence, under the immovable permanence of the cold.

"You're lying," my classmates yelled, and later
the whole class trapped me in the school attic
and beat me, screaming that I was a Jew
who believed in G-d (remember, these were Soviet times
and believing in G-d was forbidden)
and that I was lying
about the northern lights I saw in Vorkuta.

They had never seen the Northern lights, but they knew
what a Jew looked like.

A Jew looks like me.
A Jew
looks like this person with too much curly hair and an eating disorder
and too many academic degrees and too much
change, less than a model immigrant
from too many places
to too many places,
never believing that I will be heard

because people have trouble believing
that things exist that they have never seen.

Every time I open my mouth or flex my fingers to write
I am putting a brave face upon the thawing permafrost.

I am not lying. I am just
constantly changing languages, idioms, continents, genders, homes, and I
am
not even sure how to mourn from this vantage,
let alone perform any other human activity
let alone be a good
anything:
a good child, a good immigrant, a good parent, a good spouse, a good
writer
(only if I'm silent)
(squeezing my lips shut so tightly)

(clenching my fingers)
(trying to fit)
(always trying to fit)
remembering that where I'm from, a Jew
cannot be good by definition, a Jew
must become a person instead, become a Jewperson and then simply
a good Soviet citizen
but secretly a rootless cosmopolitan

who never speaks anything but the purest Russian
who eats no herring or raw garlic under any circumstances
before going out,
because everybody knows that Jews stink of those two things.

This is the one permanent axis of my identity,
that I am a Jew: that is
a rootless cosmopolitan
at home nowhere
in no language, in no country, not even among other Jews, eating
herring and garlic with a sense of deep satisfaction
that comes with the hope that, living in the Midwest,
nobody's going to surreptitiously sniff me for that
telltale stench of a Jew which
cannot be spoken of in polite society,
cannot be uprooted,
cannot be forgotten
or forgiven;
only silenced.

R. B. Lemberg

2.

My father, too, was a Jew.
After the war you eat everything, especially as an orphan:
mushrooms in the forest, bread
of any age, pork sausage
cooked by the mothers of your Ukrainian friends.

Treyf was how we made it through:

One year, grandmother Saya raised a pig.
They had nothing to eat, but it was a big deal, a part
of the family mythos:

the pig was fed at 5AM, and what it ate
was otrubi — I have no idea about the English word —
which had to be cooked an hour earlier. I did not know
what the word meant in Russian either, when I was small,
but I saw it in my mind's eye: a vat
of whitish stuff, boiling in shadow.
It was a big deal, that pig
raised by my grandmother, who never ate pork
before, who kept kosher
through Soviet times, without speaking a word of it.

She did not like my father to go over
to the neighbors', even though he was always hungry
and she was always hungry.

I wonder now how many
of these grown-ups had been perpetrators.

On the bitterest nights my father would sometimes
speak up, mocking
a woman's voice that gave instructions
to her husband: "Go over
to Ester's —
she has a sewing machine" — and his arm
made the motion of a falling axe.
That sewing machine, see,
was found at the neighbors'

after the war, and Ester
(my paternal great-grandmother)
was dead, and nothing
could be proven — the Germans did it all.

R. B. Lemberg

3.

In one life, I am a painter. I live to paint
this picture: my maternal great-grandmother
in Siberian evacuation.

It is called "To the Doctor."

Roza is a big-bodied woman in a torn, patched coat,
disheveled hair flying from under the kerchief, steering
an old sleigh through the darkening winter wood.

The composition is dynamic:

thin galloping horses, the roan
keeps looking back, its eyes round with terror, teeth bared
at the hungry shadows and the snow.
Roza clutches the whip
with that power that rises from within
in the screaming hour and is solid,
and around which all is centered:

because the child lies
oh the pale child lies in the sleigh under a warm coat
and there's no way to stop to check if he's still breathing
when the trees grow teeth and the roan keeps rearing

at the shadows and the wailing and the darkness and the snow.

I paint other things too,
still lives and spaceships and whatnot, but this
is my masterpiece: *K doktoru.*

I paint
my great-grandmother screaming her rage as I've screamed
at my own gaping wolves, from my own
unshakable, defiant secret core
knowing that I will never let go
for all the cold and all the wind and the hunger and the pain.

Later, an acquaintance told me
that mothers are overrepresented in media,

mothers and their protective BABBY feelings, she said,
"We need other stories already" — but no. This one is mine.

Listen, she saved him:
a dozen times, a thousand times she saved him.

Borya made it through the war. He died at thirty-six
from a heart condition
that became operable just five years later.
Roza watched him take his last breath, unable
to do anything more for him after thirty-six years of riding.

My grandmother Sofya, the surviving twin
was not so fragile (a good thing)
though she never let her fingers curl around the handle
of a whip, her breath held prisoner by frost.

How's that for a protective babby story? Shut up already,
you and all the others who told me
over and over again that I should not write, or what
I should write when I write, and how
I should write more or less like you or nothing at all because
there's either no room for me or I'm taking up too much room.

The reasons keep changing,
but the undercurrents remain,
playing out in my head like a whiff of raw garlic
that cannot be killed even with the minty fresh mouthwash;
the underlying absence where G-d has been,
unspeakable
so I won't speak of it.

Perhaps that's why I do not paint.

I tried for a long time, before my first immigration,
but my mother expected better from me
since I was a child: painting technique and mood
precise and perfect at eight, twelve, fourteen
even when we were sleeping on the floor, refugees
from the crumbling Soviet Union.

She knew other children who painted
or did math or played music
while sleeping on similar floors, but I
had too much feeling and too little technique,
so she was ashamed
to show my drawings to all these other parents
of these other perfect, talented, *thin*
immigrant children.

I have divined, I think
the secret of their success — that one ingredient I lacked
and still lack: their mothers
loved them
enough to launch a thousand sleighs through the wood, and fatten
a thousand pigs — certainly enough
to pack lunches
for their children to take to school — even an empty sandwich
if there was nothing to put on it —

and they ate

while I just stood there, watching.

There's hunger
where my mother's love should have been
still insatiable after all these decades.

Hunger is where my father and I meet.

4.

Having survived the war, my grandmother
wanted a little girl. In 1946
she dressed my father
in girl's clothing,
braided his hair with ribbons all through his infancy,
but she was mistaken:
I am the trans person here.

Sometimes I indulge
in this fantasy:
that he did not know how to be a boy —
fatherless, perpetually hungry, running
through the woods where shrapnel and armaments
were still in plain sight after the war,
where half-buried bombs detonated during play
killing war-begotten children, where

ancient carp and pikefish, laden with moss,
hid in lakes and (so the stories went)
could be caught
if one had a sturdy enough raft
held together with green vines, like my father's,

then coming apart, like his.

I remember
this feeling from my childhood, only without the bombs —
in all the wild places he showed me.

I did not know how to be a girl, and he
did not know what to do with a girl, so we did
what we liked: fishing
in the quietest places, on the lakes
and the rivers of Ukraine, where the herons
rose up from the water,
their beaks heavy with trembling silver.

The sounds of small waves lapping, the thin screech
of oars in their ukliuchiny, and then silence;
the big silence I miss so much
amidst the cacophony of languages, the calamity of my life,
the whirligig of rootlessness: that palpable feel
rising like milky mist from the river —
saying nothing
because he said nothing,
because there was no need,

together,

where nobody else could be.

5.

These two things I know:
my father is my hero,
and that he gave up
on me — on everything,
after grandmother Saya died. And then, immigration
to Israel — a blow after the mortal wound
had already been dealt.

What reason could there be in the world,
what pleasantness, what hope, when the mother
with whom you raised a pig and starved after the war,
the mother whose love filled all the gnawing absences —
grandmother Saya died

in her apartment in Berdichev, and lay there
for three days
because nobody knew.

Alone.

He certainly wasn't there — for that you need daughters,
or so I have always been told.

No, he was in Vorkuta when the telegram came.
We were home alone, he and I.

I witnessed my father break for many hours.

He broke into tiny pieces nobody could pick up, except
perhaps he expected me to
pick them up — somebody had to,

and I tried.

I was twelve, and I tried, oh I tried and tried,
but it did not change anything.

I keep picking up pieces of people since then,
picking them up and putting them back together.
People come to me, carrying pieces

in their outstretched hands, and I labor,
I labor long and hard and usually thanklessly

and that's all right, because perhaps one day
I will put my father back together, too.

But he did not ask me for that.
He did not ask me for anything.

I stopped
existing in that hour, his gaze
forever since sliding past me
into an enormous gaping absence
that no empty sandwiches could fill,
nor buttered ones, nor whole pigs, nothing.

I understand now that suddenly he needed me to be like her
not just in looks but in demeanor,
and that's a lot for any child to carry
especially after immigration,
sleeping on floors, disoriented, especially since
he never asked directly (only his eyes), especially since
he had forgotten how to talk to me, especially since
I wasn't even a girl.

6.

There are Jews from all sides
in my family: on my father's
side, devout Communists who wanted to build a better future
for everyone, even the Jews (with predictable outcomes),
on my mother's
side, the klezmer fiddlers, the imprisoned
historians,
the cobblers, the tailors. I sometimes think

that Jewishness is a condition where you must always bury
something: grief, or bodies, or gold-jewelry-and-watches —
if you have them, certainly bury these
before any occupying armies come.

Bury your loved ones. Don't get too attached
to the ones that survived — there's always something

brewing on the horizon: war, dereliction,
destruction, exile, imprisonment, despair.
Bury the letters
received from abroad after the censors shred them, bury
your books, or better yet burn them.
Bury your language. Pretend
you've always spoken with the perfect enunciation
of other people
with power over you.

It's a matter of pride now — you've never spoken anything else,
certainly nothing *parochial*, nothing
reminding anyone of anything, nothing
with that funny little accent, ending
each sentence in a question mark.

No questions remain.
If you speak about the war,
then speak of the partisans, speak of the victorious Soviet army,
speak of the evacuation if you must,
even, quietly, of your dead —

R. B. Lemberg

but the word "Jew" cannot be uttered
in this context
under any circumstances.

Most importantly,
bury your grief. Practice before the mirror and buy sunglasses
just in case, because everybody knows
that Jews have sad, haunted eyes
that are simply begging for a fist.

Bury any remaining slivers of G-d
because they told you that you must
and now you believe it:
it's only logical that when you are
gone and buried,
there is nothing.

So cheer up, dirty Jew,
soon communism will triumph everywhere
the friendship of the peoples will triumph and
end the need for peoples
and most definitely the need for Jews
who must blend in
become like everyone else
never stand out —
these rootless cosmopolitans
lurking everywhere
pretending to be other people,

which is the utmost danger of the Jew.

7.

Moving
in a straight line to the far northeast,
to the Ural Mountains where
they forced political prisoners to mine coal
and precious stones and big
chunks of rock salt (now a museum) — Vorkutlag —
the Vorkuta GULAG — that place
of ex-convicts, political or not, and/or people
looking for severnye — the extra pay
due to Soviet workers laboring in subarctic conditions — moving
halfway across the continent to escape the KGB
because you did not want to betray your friends
(but we must never speak of it)

might mean you'll never have friends again, never
allow yourself to get that close to anyone. Retreat
to the snow-guarded wooden studio with its mellow heat,
the smell of turpentine and sheets of colored glass
and silence — if you don't
have any friends,

the people in coats won't ask you to betray them.

If you leave
your child
behind
in Ukraine
to be raised by your mother-in-law

the people in coats will believe that you did not care
because they told you they knew you had this child
and that this child was four
and where you lived with this child,
and where you worked while caring about this child,
which is why you need to inform for them

and if you would agree
to inform for them
to betray your friends
you would have a solo exhibit in East Germany
with all your paintings, and so

you never complete another painting.

The hand does not know why the mind cannot.
The mind does not know why the heart keeps refusing —
not to lift the brush (you endlessly began), but to put it down
in the exact right moment, for all the decades since

except to complete work-related assignments.

I endlessly begin, too,
afraid to finish, just as my father was,
in the shadow of the same old fear.

The ghost KGB keep tabs on what is theirs:
my fear, and my father's, the knowledge that they will come
in the night,

although I am working on it.

I have more tools. I say that it is my great grace
that I have all these tools when my father had nothing
except the wooden stave
he broke off a tree in case of any danger,
because he walked on the train tracks through the night
because he had no money for the train.

I clench my fingers
around that wooden stave sometimes, or
curl them around Roza's horsewhip:

these are the expressions of my two genders, my inheritances
that did not make it
through war and migration in any material form.

8.

In the war, I am given to understand,
great-grandmother Roza stole potatoes.
This is how they survived —
my grandmother Sofya
and Borya, her twin,
stood by the pot as the water boiled.

I am given to understand
that great-great-grandmother Shprintze stood by the same stove
and she picked up the peels
of the stolen potatoes,
and made for herself some kind of latkes.

Later,
from the future of the fifties and her blindness, she yelled
Gedenk! in Yiddish, but nobody remembers
what she wanted us to remember. Sometimes
I yell *Gedenk!* when nobody can hear me; *Gedenk!*
through the thick walls of my office or in my head, and that's
all I have to remember.

Sometimes, the latkes.

R. B. Lemberg

9.

I unzip my body like a big soft sack,
looking for more things to sell —
that's how grandmother Saya survived the war.
When I was born, she wasn't fat,
just her skin, sagging over treasures sold in hunger.
A big emptiness where all had once been —
words, family, an open window with its freshly starched lace curtain,
big cherry trees that began to bloom
again after the war ended,
the sour cherries as big and bloody as a fist.

She told me, once there was a tangle of gold
rings and necklaces inside her,
watches from all the grandfathers and their dead.
In the war, they ate turnips and stale bread,
zipping and unzipping the burlap of her stomach.

I eat because I do not remember
what it's like to not live in the shadow of that war,
what it's like to have security
believing that one's house will continue to stand
unburned, believing that people live in houses
and not in the backs of carts or on the floors
of airports, at best in apartments
shared with two other families; believing
that one sleeps in beds rather than on top
of toppled armoires, or on the ground; one cannot
labor enough to escape the narrative.

This is my self-care: I unzip my skin,
take out my own treasures: a tallow candle, gold
protuberances of the sun, letters that peeled
from desecrated Torah scrolls, my lenience
towards the dirt and grime, and I put it all in poems,
or, when the guilt gets too much, into turnips:
my contribution
to the long, long recovery from the war
I have not seen, but which I am still fleeing
even as people here voted it in.

My body can't cooperate. I stop sleeping,
I eat my way through farmers markets, gift boxes,
donation boxes, the pantry, the cafeteria,
I eat my way through sleeplessness and fear
waiting for that knock on the door
or the announcement on the radio,
shuddering with every familiar turn of phrase
in languages new to me: and yet I continue

inhabiting houses, making
elaborate dishes out of turnips, I
buy ever-expanding clothes, I
do not know how to deal with all this,
I am overwhelmed, I am self-hating, I am grateful, I am prescient,
the world keeps changing in old familiar ways,
the war forever looking to return,
people cheering it on as if nobody ever
learned anything; somewhere
grandmother Saya's cherry trees are still in bloom.

I tell myself that I will go on,
I'll just keep expanding until I outgrow
even the great war and all my immigrations,
until it is safe enough to be small,

but I know that my smallness has never been safe,
has never felt right even when it was praised
for trying; and I am done
destroying myself for the sake of that anxiety
of needing to look as if nothing ever happened;
and I am strong,

knowing that I must speak of yet worse things,
zipping and unzipping the soft cavern of my stomach.

R. B. Lemberg

10.

Once, thaw came to Vorkuta.
Not even thaw yet: the thought of it in my father's mind,
rivulets of water sliding off
the impenetrable frozenness below.

It was a story from Ukraine,
where I lived with my grandmother the year prior
because *you are too sickly* (said my mother) or because
nothing (said my father) but in any case,
there was a spring ritual there, in Ukraine.

With each thaw
children would set little ships afloat in the parks —
in melting snow rivulets that ran through the brown
thawing earth downhill and out of sight
into the darkness. Every year the ships set sail.

I think they're sailing still
where we cannot see them — launched in snow-born streams and down
through the old drainage grates and down again,
into the secret underground core of the city,
the catacombs where Jews hid in the war, and yet deeper
into the slippery veins of the earth, carrying
our hopes with them —

the hopes of perished children in the war,
the hopes of the hungry, the bereft, the well-off, the unborn —
— of all of us who set the small boats free from our hands:

ships of whatever fashion
could be found: of birch bark, paper, sticks, of wood.
With my grandmother
we launched a matchstick boat downstream into the dark.
She said,
if your father was here,
he would make you a wooden ship
(it sounded like a fairytale)
more beautiful than any other child's,
and so, next year,

in Vorkuta, I bothered him.

There are no streams here, he said,
because nothing has thawed yet, and nothing
was ever going to thaw, but I said I would carry
my ship away to grandmother's. I did not understand
why he frowned so, when he sat
by the window in his studio,

an angular block of wood in his hand.

He began to carve
an elaborate, flat boat
out of that plank — it was vertical
with a narrow, flat bottom, and two tall, flat sides.

On these flat sides
of the vertical, flat boat
he chip-carved a radial pattern
strong, modernist, swirling from the center
to the sides — it was breathtaking
in any other context
except this one,

because this ship would never sail.

He did not even finish it.

I remember standing
by his chair, my heart in my throat,
not understanding
whether he misunderstood my story of the streams
or whether he made a decision
to taunt me — and I said

It will sink, and he said, How do you know?

But he knew. I knew and he knew.

I do not remember
much else, except that a friend of his came by

and my father said *here I am*
sitting and chipping away at this ship
in a voice that said, I'd rather be anywhere
else but here, and all I remember is the light
falling slantwise through the greenish glass, the snow outside
never planning on melting,
never in a thousand years, and his voice
and his shadow: as implacable as the permafrost.
Now I wonder

if there was a third option. I wonder if the wood
called out a pattern from itself, and he had no choice but to carve,
not caring about its utility, or my request
or even about me —

because in his childhood the ships had no decoration
there were no ships
and no decoration
only the gnawing hunger and the endless desiccated fields,
only the emptiness above, the emptiness below,
only the war children calling, calling from under the earth,
calling from under all cities —
so it did not matter

that his boat was flat
and unfinished: he was pushing against that,
and there was no room for much else: just push
and push with a thousand unfinished works

until he gave up, the stream
running into the grates of drainage and out of sight
with his elaborate, unfinished, heavy boat

carrying all hopes into the dark.

11.

Last year, the polar vortex
moved masses of snow south, pursuing me to Kansas
where I have been living as quietly as I could
away from everything, certainly from
the circumpolar winter and its visions of the wind
painting emptiness with both hands, painting snow's
whorls and eddies, painting the endless dance that erases us
willingly into G-d's
whiteout, erasing us
willingly into our own silence
until we are pacified; even if the polar caps have melted,
the winter within us, like an unclenched fist,
clasps inside and does not let go.

R. B. Lemberg

12.

I almost died once. On the crossing
between Vorkuta's center and our new subdivision,
forty minutes' walk by foot
after the buses stopped going
and nobody owned a car.
This was a regular route
and our regular route, even in the darkest polar night
after work and school: my mother knew
that a snowstorm had blown through;
but still we pressed on,
just the two of us.

Three snowy hills needed to be crossed:
closest to the town's center, the low tracks
of the freight railroad; then —
twenty or so minutes into the whiteness — the second
crossing
of the passenger railroad, much higher uphill,
and in the snowdrifts you had to follow the path and you had
to see, somehow, the unmarked crossing
after a snowstorm last night, swallowed by the whiteness.

Going uphill was the most terrifying thing;
you turned back and saw the town
and all of its old GULAG ghosts swirling
close to the ground, and the long
long line of your own footsteps disturbing eternity
which had fallen, and will have fallen again
blanketing your footsteps
before you descended.

Once that was over, the third
crossing was not a railroad —
a pipeline, circular, huge,
twice taller than a person, unclimbable,
that ran and ran and ran; I never saw its end.

Sometimes,

for years before and after
I dreamt of digging under it until I have burrowed my way;
I was told it carried hot water, and so
I imagined it would be warm, and I wanted to know
if there was anything under the snow,
if the permafrost could be moved, if
there was an escape from the sky, that upturned bowl of frozen
stars like shards, falling upwards and sideways, always falling.

Nobody ever had dug under it,
and people seemed surprised when I asked
and asked again so quietly that I said nothing,

it wasn't a thing you asked about, because
if you crossed the second crossing
in the right place, and followed
the path, there was a wooden bridge
that led up and over this pipe,
and in ten minutes, you were home. Otherwise

in all directions, a vast silence.

"Icicles" are bodies of people caught by snow
each winter and found in spring, when the thin
utter layer of whiteness gives way to slush.
Each spring they'd find these icicles, including at this crossing,
because it was easy to miss
when the snow fell heavy
in the dark
of the polar winter, and yes, unrelenting, the stars
tore out patches of night with their cold brightness,

The northern lights unfolded above with a greenish sheen
shimmering into blue and purple,

as if somebody had waved the sky
and waved it again
like a prayer shawl
in which to wrap the dead, changing
everything subtly, from snow to snow,
covering all the tracks.

R. B. Lemberg

And that's how we became lost

having crossed the second crossing
in the wrong place,
on the long, long walk home.

Descending that hill, my mother kept going
in the wrong direction
left, left, farther and further away
dragging me with her, not listening when I protested,
then panicking when she sank
up to her knees into the quagmire of the snow,
and then deeper,
deeper.

She stopped. She could not move.

Everything around us looked the same:
the unclimbable hill behind, the unpassable pipe
in front of us, and above us the vortex of the sky, and the snow
below, stretching down forever
into the secret core of the earth
that had swallowed the GULAG and all
its ghosts,
the snow that kept its secrets.

As always when she was terrified she looked angry.

I have not fully learned that lesson yet, but now her anger
froze into a blank rictus, her eyes
glazed. She told me later
she had a single thought, *I caused*
the child to perish, and she looked

away from me, abruptly wordless
which she never was; she always yelled
or argued, sometimes talked, but never before

silent.

Her silence made room for me.

I said I am not as heavy, I said I think
I know where we went wrong,
I said, I can find the way. She did not move,

then slowly
told me
it is not possible to find the way,
then,
after
moments,
she said,
if you want to, then go,

and without another word, I ran.

This is something you need to understand:
I am streamlined in emergencies.
I act fast,
emotionless, unerring,
picking my moves with precision, my mind
clear, and empty of anything but clarity.

It's not a virtue; it's just the way I'm wired, or perhaps
the way I rewired myself
because nobody came for me and I had
to come for all my others; and then for myself
from the vantage of thirty years later,
but I did not yet know about that.

The northern lights
above me, undulating with the sky's darkness
over a vast whiteness of the earth, and cupped
between these polarities, belonging
nowhere, I ran

and ran
sinking slightly, always moving,

in the deep snow
along the pipe's course
without hesitation, until I saw

R. B. Lemberg

the wooden crossing
rickety, all but swallowed, still there,
over that humongous unpassable pipe.

I turned and ran back.

Eternities passed

above and below me; G-d had unfolded
his prayer shawl of cold-blue and green, the sheen
of the sky's shivering heartbeat so profound and so slow,
and my existence within it:
a speck of moving gray.

When I reached her, my mother still stood
like Lot's wife, staring
not even after me —
into the circular shape of the pipe, her hand
gloveless; she put her glasses in the glove
because they froze; she said
she did not want to lose them,
not even thinking about frostbite.

Later she told me she knew she would die, and if I made it
she did not think I would return,
she knew for sure that I would not return,

perhaps remembering the moment in the wheat, but I doubt it.

I did not remember it either,
being left in the wheat,
and if I would, I still would never
leave her — leave anyone.

So I took
her hand in mine, and together
we made it to the crossing, wrapped
in her palpable fear, her fast breathing, her
erring feet, and finally, over the pipe
out of the danger,
over the deserted road,
onto the outskirts of our subdivision.

The outer streets, empty, were dun-edged and white,
the snow tamer here, the sky
no longer quite G-d's, eaten
by the jagged edges of the buildings.

She began to speak
angrily, and I was a child again,
a child of eleven who clearly couldn't
understand anything,
who couldn't be trusted at all,
much less to save her.

Sometimes in winter I feel the old frostbite clutch
my right cheek and hand, as if I am still gripping
that moment,
as if another me who wasn't so streamlined,
that lost track of direction
and resolve
for a brief, bright a moment,
that child

remained there.

Now that the permafrost is thawing, that perished
child is thawing as well.

13.

Over the years, my friends
and quite a few therapists
tried to diagnose my mother
from over the ocean,
without speaking a word of Russian, Yiddish, or Hebrew
without knowing
how she tried so hard to hide
her too-big nose, her body, her father —

her father most of all,

carted away to a GULAG —
not Vorkutlag, another
somewhere in Siberia,

where I heard he went mad, or maybe he had always been like this,
self-centered, harsh, brilliant — one could easily diagnose him too

from the far-off safety of a therapist's office in the US where
a tree never falls in the snow-deep silence of the taiga
felled by the convicts' hands, where

no sound can be made: and no sound has been made
of my grandfather's life:

I do not know much about it
except that he composed
a dictionary of Russian synonyms
as a prisoner of the GULAG, over and over,
in Russian, even though he was a polyglot.

I have written a story about this.
I have written a dozen, because I have nothing,
not even a creak of that collapsing tree.

How does it help now to diagnose my mother, when
at thirteen
she saw her father
for the first time; repressed in the Stalinist camps

somewhere in Siberia,
it took him thirteen years to be able to contact them.
She remembers

circling and circling the bench where my grandparents sat
in some town far away from Ukraine but
not far from the GULAG —
where the ex-cons were allowed to settle.

He repeated, over and over,
What a fool I've been.

And my mother circled,

What a fool. What a fool I've been

— but he abandoned them even after that,
or perhaps it was mutual; my grandmother Sofya
unable to abide his fits of jealous rage
inspired by nothing, because she had waited
for him, for thirteen years;
and waited, as I know all too well,
for all the long decades after
despite an endless parade of suitors.
She waited —
not for him anymore, but for that moment

never to have existed
backwards and forwards,
the future again pristine as the untouched snow.

When she passed away, the snow still lay thick
over all the GULAG sites, but I have no such luck;

my mind is forever thawing, and all the dead with it.
The muddy water the only thing that can be seen,

and all my dead whisper, "This is not it."
They whisper in English, even if they don't know it.
In other languages they only shake their heads —
"This is not it, what you're writing,
this is not the snow we remember."

I remember

coming to Vorkuta when I was six,
barely recognizing my father's face after two years away.
My mother joked about it; she was only
away for a year, so that was nothing. It was all nothing,
they were only away for a short time: not years,
definitely not
forever. Perhaps they felt that
going away was what all parents did.

But: *We made a dragon for you,* they told me.

It was a whole playground chiseled out of frozen ice.
I did not understand, but they did — it was their project
commissioned for the beautification of the city
of Vorkuta, its crowning glory
an enormous reclining dragon,
a slide for the children to slide off: all ice.

We made it for you. This is how their love manifested:

in public,
for the whole city to see,
and secretly for me;
and they got angry when I did not understand
how it could be for me,
when they took me there. I remember

dozens of children sliding off the dragon,
the enormous frozen dragon I see in dreams sometimes —
the other children pushing me away, to slide off its back, laughing

and their parents waited below
waited to catch them
under the cogwheel of the six-month-long polar night.

Their parents' love
was simple — not an epic dominion of carved ice, and so
they had no need for these stories, no need for these languages, these

names,
these words, these peregrinations, these publications, these hesitations,
these tears, this memory, these doubts, this guilt, this shame, no need
for the enormous scintillating dragon
that would weep into the earth with the thawing permafrost,
except that the city razed it
in the spring, while it was still cold.

In dreams, sometimes
I lay on the dragon's curved back, looking up
at all the unblinking stars, myriads of them,
the sky's so black and so clear, you can see through the whole universe
towering above — an endless tunnel of stars, ascending
into G-d's endless, unfathomable core. And I am waiting

for the thawing permafrost to catch its breath, I'm waiting
to look up through the universe and see G-d again, I'm waiting

for the dead to come back. My father
in his forties, still strong, only beginning
to be furled by heart disease.

I dream of him talking to me — talking
like he never did; or simply being there,
a chisel in his hand, or dipping his brush
into turpentine — he used to tease me, say
the turpentine was my tears
because the permafrost was never my domain.

I fear
that when the dead return, they will bring
their armor back with them:
their secrets, their subterfuges, their jokes,
their silenced languages, their brokenness — and underneath it, love
as permanent as the snow. What he knew about it.

14.

Whenever I'm sick, and I am often sick,
the deaths of my loved ones haunt me.
My father's great heart refusing him at last
after so many bare survivals; grandmother Saya
lying cold in her cold apartment,
grandmother Sofya, screaming
from the room where I used to sleep, my father —
holding her hand till the last
like he couldn't for his own mother, who died
cold in her cold apartment — he held
grandmother Sofya's hand while I lay in the other room,
speaking faster and faster in all the languages I could
make up, to tune it out;

I wasn't fast enough — not then,
not since.

My grandfather
— the one who'd been a fool —
I do not know how he died, but I dream
of the convicts that fell
in the taiga,
with only the trees to hear them.

The dead fall in slow motion towards the center of gravity,
the center of clarity, the Center of All Things, the silence
of snow and wind; G-d's
endlessness. I am not ready
to climb the winding stair that leads past the places
where my loved ones let go
of the railing, where they fell,
despairing of everything, eyes
pursed so tightly; I feel it, sometimes,

that leaden weight, that wind, that cold, that fear.
My fingers open and close on that railing
whenever I'm sick, and I am often sick.

15.

Here is a hard thing to remember
but I must write of it, because
it holds a key to everything:

once
I was left
in the wheat.

We were vacationing in rural Ukraine
my parents and my grandmother Sofya and I
as we did every summer after
my parents moved to Vorkuta, reunited
in the landscape of forest and river and seed
renting a small house
in some village whose name escapes me.

And we walked to town and we were coming back
through a large field. The sun was bearing down,
and from behind, the dark shadows of the forest, and ahead, more trees,
the house somewhere beyond that. I

felt

unwell.

I was a child of six and sickly and often
I would fall ill suddenly. They all knew it.

I told my mother
that I could not walk anymore.

Imagination suggests
that my father offered to carry me,
but I think he said nothing.

I was very unwell and my mother said
that if I was throwing a tantrum
and refusing to walk
then I had to stay behind.
And my father said nothing,

so I lay down
in the wheat.

I remember lying there
among the golden stalks, the sun bearing down, feeling
the old wet earth under me, the same earth I keep leaving
and returning to,
and teaching Bashevis's *Slave* brings back the rustling and the golden
glow of these places, the deep sense of alienation, as if a slice of me
was cut and forever planted
like a sliver of stone, into that earth,
like a river that dries up but still continues to be named,
like a language: but I had no such language
because I was six.

I was lying
just lying
just lying there

eventually
I gathered some strength to sit up
and look
over the wheat.

On a winding road in the distance, my mother
flanked by my grandmother and my father, were walking away
so small in the distance.
I saw their backs. Still moving.

I do not know how I forced myself to run.

They did not stop so I kept running
silently crying (I never threw a tantrum, then or since)
and the dust and the heat and the pounding of my blood

and the sweet pain spreading through every limb, whispering

that all who survived pushed through and all who didn't
are buried in this very earth

hundreds of years, hundreds of years their bodies piling up and I
was running over them

pounding on their unmarked graves

When I caught up, my mother
began to berate me and my grandmother
put her soft, soft hand on my forehead and said,
"She is burning up."

I forced myself to push it all away
into the deepest recesses, but now
I ask myself to think of it again:

that neither of them turned back when my mother said keep walking,
that my father left and left and left and left and left
and left when he could have said no,

that if I stayed there, in the wheat,
because I could not move,
they would not have come back, that still
after all these decades, these immigrations,

I keep running, I keep running after them
and they're not looking back;

and still, after all these decades, these lives, these languages, these words,
this wisdom, these accomplishments, this pain,
I keep running:

still feverish, still crying, still hoping they would come for me, but

nobody's coming.

16.

Nobody's coming. Like ghosts, they flit around
demanding to be heard, demanding
to exist — demanding my obedience
to the unspoken rules
of their deeply felt world
with its thousands of conflicting social cues

about what can be said and to whom
about our Jewishness, understanding
that I must not complain,
that my silence, one step above my nonexistence
is what was being sought — understanding
compassionately
that leaving a sick child behind

was imperative: that even if I died there
in the wheat
it was an act of love. So never

throw any tantrums, never
disobey any spoken or unspoken rules,
be streamlined in emergencies, write
something but not *this*, excel —
ALWAYS EXCEL —
in everything. Speak purer Russian
than the Russians, solve
even the hardest math problems without hesitation
because the entrance exams
to any university
have a tougher set of problems given only to Jews.

Don't trust anyone. Trust family
to know what's best, even if they leave you, understand
that you haven't been and will never be free,
that if/when the war comes, you will not survive

and they know it. Parent birds

lift one gosling from the endangered nest

leaving the rest behind.
They move fast and without hesitation; they've made
an unspoken agreement
to save another child; and every time
they want to get attached to you
they know it.

R. B. Lemberg

17.

I remember the leaving year
dimly; the Soviet Union was breaking, and my father
broken in his grief. We were back
in Ukraine, because
we were going to leave, and grandmother Saya
was gone, and grandmother Sofya
had cancer. You could not say
the word *cancer* — only obliquely,
like any other word that brought bad luck.

She did not know about the cancer yet, but every night
sleeping by her side on the sofa-bed, I dreamt of her dying.
I woke up screaming, in cold sweat, and she couldn't
understand, and said she couldn't, and I couldn't
speak of it. My father

said he would walk with me. At 5am
he woke me up to walk with him through the pre-dawn streets
of L'viv, and every lantern
flared to life as we passed, stealing shadows
from the ancient gnawed streets of the city; he joked

that I wouldn't want to come, that I wouldn't
wake up, but I was eager
to follow him into the dark streets with their smell
of dawn being born in the stone,

to follow him anywhere —
and he strode forward

without saying a word or looking back.

We went out twice, and then he refused
to wake up early even one more time —

because he wanted to sleep, or because
he could not finish anything, or because
I wasn't important enough to walk with,
or maybe nothing was

important, beyond that moment
in the dim Vorkuta corridor
two years ago when the telegram came,
when he stopped
seeing me, when his gaze
started sliding

so early yet, before the final dark.

18.

I thought my city flowed through me,
making its currents my own,
claiming me with each and every stone sigh
as its sigil, its sentience: so that I would be its shadow
falling on the cobblestones before dawn
when the light spills jagged from the lantern, that I would walk
steps echoing and my city in me,
hurrying to catch up
with that lean tall shadow I thought I followed,
following only myself: but I was yanked out of my city.

What was left to me? What corner of the world
would give me refuge? I thought another city would take me in,
speak its voice through me, unravel its truths
through my bumbling voice: wet stones by the ocean,
bookstores that closed and yet remain
accessible to those with enough conviction; a speakeasy
hiding behind a staircase — but I would find no solace there,
no longer believing in cities and shadows.

In America, my house
stands in a row of houses resting
on rain-soaked ground. One day the rain will sweep me too,
carry me gently with the slow rotting leaves,
carry me until there is nothing to carry.

19.

During that last year in Ukraine, my parents went
on a guided tour of East Germany,
their first foray abroad
from the sagging Soviet Union. My father
saw a piece of leather luggage in the shop window in Berlin;
he said it was leather, masculine and refined, he said
he'd never wanted things, but then he saw this. The store
was closed, and even if it wasn't,
it was unlikely that he'd buy it with Soviet money, but he sighed
wistfully, when he came back

and spoke of it. I was thirteen, and I imagined
traveling with this luggage when the time came,
pensive and dreamy and clutching old books, but we
fled. Even the tin
of buttons was packed away in a crate —
all the buttons cut from the grandmothers' old dresses,
and grandmother Sofya's
death certificate was ten days old.
They put us

on a one-way train to Budapest.

Grandmother Sofya's ghost
struggled to follow us, but lost her way
somewhere in the fields between point A
and the warehouse. A plastic bag
of old photographs. A dry salami.
In Hungary, they put us behind bars.

I remember the holding
space. It was enormous, echoing; a warehouse
or an old gym; under the eaves
there must have been pigeons; I only heard them.
Someone's grandmother —
she looked about ninety — sat forlornly
on one of the many plain beds.
She looked so lost there, but I was afraid
to come closer. My own grandmother

was sixty-five, just ten days ago.
She will forever be
sixty-five, not a year more, while the years keep coming.

There were narrow windows
high by the ceiling, and bars
on these windows. My father said,

let's see
if we can flee

first just the two of us, out of this place,
find an American embassy,
but his heart wasn't in it, and we already knew
that America wasn't receiving;
they had quotas.

So when the soldier
stopped us by the barred door, my father
who wasn't ever afraid, became timid
and turned back inside without much argument.

Arguing wouldn't have helped anyway, but he didn't, and they didn't
let us peek out. My father said
Budapest must be beautiful.

In Israel, the Gulf War
is the first thing I remember. Bombs falling, and a gaping
hole in the wall. Sirens. You had to have
a "sealed room," but the room
we had had a hole in it, so we
locked ourselves in the bathroom. The gas mask smelled
like gas, or burnt rubber,

or a language.

Cockroaches ate
my mother's salvaged wedding dress, and I learned
to speak; made up three languages to hide in.

20.

I remember my father standing
standing with a crowbar

      — it was Sukkot, almost
a full year after we arrived —

my father standing
with a crowbar, under the overflowing sun.

I remember his arm lifting up. He was prying
apart the wooden slats of the shipment crate,
the single crate we were allowed to ship from Ukraine
to Israel — and finally here. He pried

the wooden slats one by one,

slowly, because he knew
and I knew: the wooden shell
of the crate had already been broken,

like a tortoise dropped by the eagle
hurtling to the ground.
(Around us, the neighbors gathered
to watch.) Almost nothing was left

unstolen or undamaged in transit: my father's
chess set, his chess
clock, my great-grandmother Roza's
buttons in the round cookie tin: all gone.
My father's
carving tools remained; the Book
of Tasty and Healthy Food, with Stalin's foreword,
and a small carpet. I remember
how my grandmother's powder case

rolled out of the crate. It had been
so beautiful once, enameled peacock blue
with glimpses of white and yellow on its honored place
on her dresser; not into powder

or makeup, I nevertheless loved its tiny
filigreed feet; and now it rolled
down the sidewalk, and it was
filthy crusted sticky besmirched — my mother
threw it away; she could not bear
to even touch it. A crowd

of Israeli neighbors stood watching around us and
with every wooden plank my father pried, a person
came near and asked him for it:

for a sukkah, they said,

and nothing else, nor offered
help, or any consolation.

Later, when we stood
orphaned in our cockroach-studded flat,
This country will be the end of me, my father said
for the first time,

twenty-five years before the last.

21.

I found a truce
with my mother a few years ago:
not because she changed, but because I have
let go of something
so vital, so deep; but I can no longer hold it.
She speaks
incessantly. *In the cemetery I did not have*
any matches — I forgot, well, I think —
I must go home to get them,
I wanted to light a candle,
so I walked — are you listening? — down some path,
back to the car — and there it was,
somebody else's matchbox
on the middle of the path — can you believe it? She never
listens to anything. *I know it's hard to believe,*
but there it was. In the middle of the road.
She asks about my child
briefly — this was my condition
for continuing to call — but quickly
changes the subject. About my partner, the same.
She had asked all the questions
when we were still "good friends," still stealth, still concerned
about tourist visas and student visas and people who call you
to ask questions about *intent to immigrate,*
and being seen together, and DOMA — but my mother
stopped asking after I told her.
Have you checked with the doctor?
she said about my queer love, as if any doctor
could unqueer me, and then
her silence covered it all.
Father could never be told
or he would die, she'd said. And now
I found a matchbox — it has rained all day yesterday —
but, would you believe it, it was dry,
as if someone put it there just for me
as if by magic — so I lit the candle.
It kindled from first attempt — are you listening?
I thought you'd understand. The dead
have eclipsed the living long ago,

if there was ever any competition. In Israel, in Jewish custom,
a stone is put on the grave, but my mother has
her candle and her flowers and the road, wet from yesterday's rain
that falls all around the dry matchbox,
my mother's magic. Only this.

22.

There is a language in things; once, as a child in Ukraine,
I found a small brass triptych tucked into the corner of
the cabinet at the base of the bookcase.
I remember the tactile feel of the dark
polished wood opening under my fingers, the rustle
of the thin plastic bag; the cool dusty touch
of brass, and the sound: a light screeching
of the flat metal cover, opening up
into a Nativity scene; the left
brass pane was missing. An old triptych with two parts,
a diptych really, but the hinges
of the missing piece
were curious to the touch. I felt

for the first time in my life, an acute
passion: a flaring
sense of urgency; I wanted

to possess something this beautiful, I couldn't
understand why my parents would hide it, I couldn't
imagine daring to ask for it for myself, or admitting
to snooping, I dreamt

of the day my parents would die
so I could inherit it —
so sudden, so old, and so desperately beautiful it was that I couldn't
imagine another moment in which it could be mine. That desire,
so acute and desolate, swept through me and I couldn't
sleep, until with an effort of will
I pushed it out of my mind.

A few years ago
I told my mother I had once found it; and she said
that it was given to my father, in the museum where he worked
in art restoration,
because it could not be repaired,
but what, we would display it? No,
it was too Christian,
and she did not know what to do about it.

R. B. Lemberg

I did not understand
back then; not really distinguishing
one forbidden religion from the other, having glimpsed
Jewish and Christian history through the same
art history books
in my parents' bookcase; but I knew beauty.

Of all the things to perish in our move —
the memories, the books, the dresses, the buttons,
my father's art, keepsakes, clothes — the brass
diptych survived. I do not know

if I'll want it again; things
are not as important now as they once were, before
the destruction of most things, before
the war, the pogroms, the revolution, the immigrations, before

I knew of all the treasures lost, and lost
a share of treasures; but I filled
my house in Kansas
with etched brass and the thin rustle of plastic wrap,

longing for that purest, wild longing
before my world was cracked askew.

23.

In Israel, my mother took my father to rabbis,
believing him to be cursed.

She visited charlatans she found in a Russian newspaper
and Orthodox rabbis certified
by some board or another:
why is he always sick? But she didn't
want answers; she wanted miracles.

Given the sudden possibility of G-d,
or rather, the sudden
open availability of G-d
after our immigration
and the fall of the Soviet Union,

she felt that G-d owed her —
and all the rabbis, owed her
to make it so the hurts would be erased;
a husband
who did not need to haul the burden of his dead

the way he hauled refrigerators
up six flights of stairs, to earn even a little
because we were sleeping on the floor
in a room with a gaping hole in the wall and
G-d owed us something.

This story I heard as a child in Vorkuta:

that they forced the political prisoners to work in construction
of the new mining and metallurgy institute.
There was this chemist, a genius
made to work day and night,
he and the others,
even in the coldest winter, or when the summer's harsh heat
awakened a thousand mosquitoes accustomed
to reindeer but preferring
the thinner human skin; he was told
to glaze the building with protective paint
against corrosion, and he did something

to that glaze,
but not what they wanted.

Again and again they painted over the building,
but every year, in the polar summer
the paint itself corrodes, eaten from inside by salt.

There is nothing to be done: the clammy walls,
in remembrance of those silenced in all the other ways
even as the snow recedes,
are weeping.

Cursed.
And my mother believed my father to be cursed,

why else would he fall silent and sicken,
why else would he lose
his will to live, and yet hang on so desperately?

This land, he said, will be the end of me, but immigration
came after he already ended
in that Vorkuta hallway
after the telegram.

His eyes, forever far away,
a curse that no rabbi could break:

that my father hung on, but at the same time disbelieved
his own living
like the wall that weeps salt.

24.

I think I was twenty-one
and visiting from college
when the phone call came. Uncle Arkady
my father's older brother,
who lived in Germany by then,
had died.

I'd seen Arkady only once. He was
thirteen years older than my father,
a pre-war child and long gone
by the time my father was five — Arkady served
in the Soviet Army, always elsewhere, and we never saw him;
few letters were exchanged. He had no part
in all the stories, and I could not understand

why my father now sat
bent over the kitchen table
clutching his head in his hands.

This was in Israel — the kitchen was small, clean, white,
and I was standing right there,
and he lifted his head and looked
at me, past me, in that familiar way
and said, vsyo proigrano
with so much pain:

everything's lost.

Translations betray me. Not *lost* like misplaced, but *lost*
like a game of chess,
a game of life — there's no more chances: vsyo proigrano.

He was looking right at me when he said it,
without seeing me, and I wanted to say,

how can all be lost when I am right here,
but there was no point and so
I just stood there, absorbing the blow
into my body, where I hold it still.

It took me decades to know
that they all loved the dead
more than the living.
The dead are safer to love:
dressed in the finery of grief
and memory, not offering any more
chances of loss, they are
always with you. Untouchable. Safe.

25.

I saw on the news that the permafrost
in the Arctic is thawing so quickly
it's leaving
sinkholes
in the decaying cadaver of the earth. And with that sinking
my whole life is untruthed. Memory
morphs. There are people here who insist
that I am American,
born here somewhere, except that nobody remembers,
to third-gen parents
in New York or California — somehow without any record, just like
nothing is thawing anywhere, the whole frozen layer of it
and all its prisoners, their stories
dying again into this new muck of an ending,
swallowed into the bewildered, unbound earth.
In Ukraine, universes ago,
my classmates did not believe me
that the permafrost was real in Vorkuta, and now it's not:

The truth itself is cratering.

My mother
does not agree that she refused my child,
her only grandchild, despite observable facts
that she only saw him twice
in his life,
before the diagnosis.

A friend asked me, reading this manuscript,
to speak more about my own parenting —
surely the thaw is evident in it,
in all of us so hurt — don't we unfreeze
these orphaned bits of us, piece by a suddenly raw piece,
to nourish our own children?

Here is my truth: the tale
of my parenting is my child's to tell
if he will ever speak or write
this story, or any other, if he would be

burdened by it, like I am,
burdened by these collapses of memory,
the sinkholes, the languages, this landslide in which the world
is once again its own event horizon;
let him write of it then. It is not my story.
My story is I screwed up plenty
and feel the heaviness of it;
I screwed up even love, at first.

In a never-developed photograph taken
by a friend's friend with an old Leica camera
despite my protestations,
I lift the newborn, my face ashen after sixty-five hours of labor
and before that, nine months
of non-stop dysphoria; I have never
felt so unambiguously, overwhelmingly a man — my two genders
usually more balanced. And I wanted
my truth, but I also wanted
a child to redeem all the death, all the dereliction,
I wanted a child after my father's first stroke, and that wasn't
the right wanting, it was too much wanting
to prison myself with, but the child
came to me nonetheless. And my first impulse

was to push

away like they pushed, with all the same subterfuges.
But then I knew: this child
who does not talk or move
like other children —
I held him
like I hadn't been, and it wasn't
about me; a little about G-d.

Inside,
within the masses of my body, signs
of cracking ice. The shifting of polarities.
The long
slide downwards.

        I remember

clutching Roza's horsewhip through all the sleepless nights, then learning
to unclutch it. Letting the light
melt her dark forest, the horses, the wolves,
even the whip, into that endless slow motion
of pivot: and life goes on

without repair those days. Just these avalanches
that leave the earth cratered, just these abrupt
swings between frozenness and the abandon
of heat, this love that melts
all words into the sun and leaves us there, holding
to each other so tightly,
in the cradle of all births and the last breath.

26.

In Vorkuta, when I was ten,
my father told me this story:
                a man
walked the streets in Arctic winter
without any gloves on. He'd been tortured in the GULAG
decades prior, and since then he couldn't
feel the cold; but only in his hands.

The rest of him was bundled like the others
in a sheepskin tulup, big hat, fur boots,
three pairs of trousers.

And he was cheerful, greeting
the shocked newcomers,
greeting my father as he hurried on,
bare-handed through the endless polar night.

I never saw this man, but I think of him now
as Kansas freezes and unfreezes
endlessly in winter, the clutch
of extreme weather going from autumn pleasantness
to blizzards in a span of a breath:
my hands, more often than not, are gloveless.

Why won't you put your gloves on, ask my partner, my therapist,
and I don't know what I'm doing, or how to explain

the comfort in pain of that old frostbite rising
to the surface of my skin, and how my hands clench
stiff around the old words, the pain
dull, sharp, dull again
twenty times this winter.
And I'm not cheerful but I know that gloved
I wouldn't be writing this,
or writing anything. I'd be

absorbed into this world, integrated
into society, into
this wet, stagnant ground
like the permafrost is thawing.

27.

Those days, Vorkuta is
the fastest-emptying city in Europe.
Winter grasps and fizzles. The townspeople
leave for the south. There is no other direction.
The endless apartment buildings
rows upon rows in the old Soviet subdivisions stand empty,
or barely occupied and impossible to heat,
so the city closes down
the buildings street by street,
neighborhood by neighborhood,
relocating all that remain
and repeat again; pipes burst, in flood-freeze cycles
like screamed waves
or stalagmites.

This was my old apartment building,
the stairway where I would run out
after a fight with my mother,
trying to flee, but it was too cold.
This was the kitchen where once
I looked out to the tundra in bloom.

Most people I know
have a more tangible childhood.
An old playground, a school, a reunion,
a yearbook. A cleaved tree
around the corner. All I know
that there was a spaceship waiting for me
at the foot of the Ural Mountains
out there, in the distance. In the blue and pink light.

The end began
innocently enough — they closed
the coal mines in the early nineties,
among them Khalmer-Yu, a small mining town where my father
had installed, just a few years prior,
a carved space divider for the miners' cafeteria:
it was made of dozens of square panels
of light-colored wood, carved in intricate

radial designs — a year of work, or more,
in stark darkness, and then the incessant slanted light
of polar summer; but everything thaws.

This was my father's great work.
Who knows what happened to it? Everything was stolen
or sold off,
or left to decay and rot.
Perhaps it is still there, a ghost of his life, his art
in the ghost town of Khalmer-Yu.
My mother has
a photograph somewhere,
but she isn't sharing.

28.

When I was a child in Vorkuta,
rocketships bloomed between my palms like dandelions.
Launched, they hovered in the air before take-off
as if they'd still cling to me; but they couldn't
and I couldn't.
I have it on good authority
that many reached the stars, populated them
with pollen cosmonauts I made from the tundra in bloom
that clings to thin life above the chasm of permafrost.
If we ever leave Earth I think we'll find them
blooming as desperately on exoplanets
having thawed a shallow ledge with my heat.

29.

been casting two shadows for as long as I remember myself
through all my peregrinations, dragging them from country to country
sleeping on airport floors, crossing borders on trains that smell of dirt and
black tea
my two shadows had a single passport between them

two student visas one training grant one work visa one very battered green
card forty-three years

one shadow got naturalized but then was voter-suppressed
one shadow went to vote and was turned away
two shadows moved six more times
together they hatched a plan to stay put
between the three of us I was outvoted
it's a good thing we didn't suppress each other
so I put down roots, tentatively
in a house that rests under the pin oaks and the sweetgum
in a house with rickety doors that smells of dirt and black tea

got them a shovel and a rake
these days
I hear my two shadows planting
strawberries in the back yard when I am trying to write

I will cast a shade garden if I move again
not knowing what grows there
two shadows five trees six trees many flowers broken trees empty lake dead
birds live birds big stones small pebbles earthworms rain slivers night

I wake up to the sound of a freight train in the distance
a ghost of the Moscow-Vorkuta line
calling me
calling me
in the lost land of my America

there's nowhere to flee
no place left to go

30.

By the time my father died
twenty-five years after the immigration,
my mother believed the whole family cursed, and kept

punishing G-d in her small desperate ways:
not lighting
Shabbat candles, which she began to light
after our arrival; eating small bits of pork
after twenty-five years of keeping kosher:

certainly my father would
get better, I would be unqueered
and married to a wealthy white American,
my child — unseen by her — begin to talk —

but nothing happened.

No miracles — just, as before,
a gaping absence where G-d had briefly been.

One day
I got a terse email. Snow had fallen

while he was in the hospital, the snow
stretching from Kansas to Chicago,
the snow,
unruly winds
the snow,
which left circumpolar Russia and came
to me instead, and clutched
all the roads and the railroads and the plane routes
as desperately as he clutched;
and he could not let go

for days after that second, final stroke, and I couldn't
bridge that distance. I could have
abandoned everything and without looking back, run
at that first news,
towards the car and drove

through the impassable blizzard, risking everything
to get to the airport in Chicago, board that flight,
but I was no longer twelve and I could not
do it, could not
travel for a long, full day
while he was dying across the ocean —

because of the snow
that receded everywhere
and came to me.

That night as he lay gasping in the hospital, I saw

the small fish leaping
from the morning milk of the river,
multicolored translucent shapes
full of solace, just like thirty years ago
when we fished on the river; and I heard
grandmother Saya's voice, calling;
the voice of the currents and the air
sparkling above all the darkening spaces.
It's all right to let go, I whispered into that place.
It's all right to let go. I do not believe it
for myself, but I gave him that.

While I was traveling from America, my mother

wrapped my father in a sheepskin tulup;
she got a special dispensation
from the morgue's rabbi, citing our custom:

because he came from Vorkuta and
the tulup came from Vorkuta and
it is the warmest thing and

he could not get warm

31.

I think
that even that cold will claw its way
to softness once; the cold where they keep all the dead.

They wait while the children are traveling
still exiles, still uprooted, still traveling

even though nowhere is safe
and you cannot trust anything,
not even the permafrost, which at this very moment

recedes, making room
for Russian military fortifications.

With my whole soul I try to make sense of this history,
wanting to trust its fall through the thawing permafrost

into the warm core of the earth,
and all its living and the dead
where G-d or my father would finally lift me

from the wheat; and interpret my history
to me in small unraveling threads
in all of our tongues and all our loves that we must have forgotten

in the place where the long pain gives way
to the small leap of the river;
but these days, still

I must pick myself up, I must

I must get up and run

even with my dead's and the living's
disapproval of everything that makes me —

my body, my life, my life's work, my history
which is their own, but I have spoken things
which should have been left unspoken, like the salt:

R. B. Lemberg

my languages, my loves, my longing.

You cannot trust anything, but here I am,
lying on my back on the ice dragon, staring
up at G-d's well of stars, still falling

into my own thaw;
the penultimate breath of the sky.

2017-2021
Lawrence, Kansas

Acknowledgments

#9 first appeared as "Eating Disorder Doesn't Begin to Describe it," in *Uncanny Magazine's* Issue 30: Disabled People Destroy Fantasy.

#18 first appeared as "Insomnia," in *Glitter*ship*, Winter 2020

#28 first appeared as "Pollen" in *Mithila Review*, 2017

I am grateful to so many readers and friends who showed up for me and for this manuscript. Thank you to Larry Yudelson and the poetry readers at Ben Yehuda Press, and especially to my editor Julia Knobloch - it has been a pleasure to work with you. Many thanks to Lisa M. Bradley, who read the manuscript with great care and gave me excellent feedback. Thank you to Sonya Taaffe, who read the book at its various stages. I trusted you when you said it was good, more than I could ever trust myself. Gratitude to Izzy Wasserstein, for her feedback and friendship. Endless appreciation to my spouse Bogi Takács, who read and commented on the poems piecemeal and together over the years, and kept me going. Thanks to Keffy M. Kehrli and Lisa M. Bradley (again) for publishing two poems from the cycle in *Glitter*ship* and *Uncanny's Disabled People Destroy Fantasy*, respectively. So many thanks to my patrons on Patreon, who followed this journey along as it unfolded. Your support means so much to me. Thank you to the members of the Lawrence Jewish Community Center, who listened to me read from the very beginning of this project in 2018 — your positive reaction stayed with me, and helped me finish the book. Finally, to my birth family, without whom none of this would exist. Multiple things can be true at the same time. Love and devastation. Anger and tenderness. They are here.

About the Author

R.B. Lemberg is a poet, fantasist, and professor living in Lawrence, Kansas. R.B.'s LGBTQIA+ focused fantasy books were shortlisted for the Nebula, Locus, World Fantasy, Crawford, and other awards. R.B. was born in L'viv, Ukraine, and also lived in subarctic Russia and Israel before migrating to the US. Follow them on twitter at @rb_lemberg or visit their website http://rblemberg.net.

R. B. Lemberg

The Jewish Poetry Project

Ben Yehuda Press

From the Coffee House of Jewish Dreamers: Poems of Wonder and Wandering and the Weekly Torah Portion by Isidore Century

"Isidore Century is a wonderful poet. His poems are funny, deeply observed, without pretension." – *The Jewish Week*

The House at the Center of the World: Poetic Midrash on Sacred Space by Abe Mezrich

"Direct and accessible, Mezrich's midrashic poems often tease profound meaning out of his chosen Torah texts. These poems remind us that our Creator is forgiving, that the spiritual and physical can inform one another, and that the supernatural can be carried into the everyday."
—Yehoshua November, author of *God's Optimism*

we who desire: Poems and Torah riffs by Sue Swartz

"Sue Swartz does magnificent acrobatics with the Torah. She takes the English that's become staid and boring, and adds something that's new and strange and exciting. These are poems that leave a taste in your mouth, and you walk away from them thinking, what did I just read? Oh, yeah. It's the Bible."
—Matthue Roth, author, *Yom Kippur A Go-Go*

Open My Lips: Prayers and Poems
by Rachel Barenblat

"Barenblat's God is a personal God—one who lets her cry on His shoulder, and who rocks her like a colicky baby. These poems bridge the gap between the ineffable and the human. This collection will bring comfort to those with a religion of their own, as well as those seeking a relationship with some kind of higher power."
—Satya Robyn, author, *The Most Beautiful Thing*

Words for Blessing the World: Poems in Hebrew and English by Herbert J. Levine

"These writings express a profoundly earth-based theology in a language that is clear and comprehensible. These are works to study and learn from."
—Rodger Kamenetz, author, *The Jew in the Lotus*

Shiva Moon: Poems by Maxine Silverman

"The poems, deeply felt, are spare, spoken in a quiet but compelling voice, as if we were listening in to her inner life. This book is a precious record of the transformation saying Kaddish can bring. It deserves to be read. These are works to study and learn from."
—Howard Schwartz, author, *The Library of Dreams*

is: heretical Jewish blessings and poems
by Yaakov Moshe (Jay Michaelson)

"Finally, Torah that speaks to and through the lives we are actually living: expanding the tent of holiness to embrace what has been cast out, elevating what has been kept down, advancing what has been held back, reveling in questions, revealing contradictions."
—Eden Pearlstein, aka eprhyme

Texts to the Holy: Poems
by Rachel Barenblat

"These poems are remarkable, radiating a love of God that is full bodied, innocent, raw, pulsating, hot, drunk. I can hardly fathom their faith but am grateful for the vistas they open. I will sit with them, and invite you to do the same."
—Merle Feld, author of A Spiritual Life.

The Sabbath Bee: Love Songs to Shabbat
by Wilhelmina Gottschalk

"Torah, say our sages, has seventy faces. As these prose poems reveal, so too does Shabbat. Here we meet Shabbat as familiar housemate, as the child whose presence transforms a family, as a spreading tree, as an annoying friend who insists on being celebrated, as a woman, as a man, as a bee, as the ocean."
—Rachel Barenblat, author, The Velveteen Rabbi's Haggadah

All the Holes Line Up: Poems and Translations
by Zackary Sholem Berger

"Spare and precise, Berger's poems gaze unflinchingly at—but also celebrate—human imperfection in its many forms. And what a delight that Berger also includes in this collection a handful of his resonant translations of some of the great Yiddish poets." — Yehoshua November, author of God's Optimism and Two World Exist

How to Bless the New Moon: The Priestess Paths Cycle and Other Poems for Queens
by Rachel Kann

"To read Rachel Kann's poems is to be confronted with the possibility that you, too, are prophet and beloved, touched by forces far beyond your mundane knowing. So, dear reader, enter into the 'perfumed forcefield' of these words—they are healing and transformative."
—Rabbi Jill Hammer, co-author of The Hebrew Priestess

Into My Garden: Prayers
by David Caplan

"The beauty of Caplan's book is that it is not polemical. It does not set out to win an argument or ask you whether you've put your tefillin on today. These gentle poems invite the reader into one person's profound, ambiguous religious experience."
— *The Jewish Review of Books*

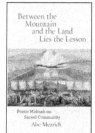

Between the Mountain and the Land is the Lesson: Poetic Midrash on Sacred Community by Abe Mezrich

"Abe Mezrich cuts straight back to the roots of the Midrashic tradition, sermonizing as a poet, rather than ideologue. Best of all, Abe knows how to ask questions and avoid the obvious answers."
—Jake Marmer, author, *Jazz Talmud*

NOKADDISH: Poems in the Void
by Hanoch Guy Kaner

"A subversive, midrashic play with meanings—specifically Jewish meanings, and then the reversal and negation of these meanings."
—Robert G. Margolis

An Added Soul: Poems for a New Old Religion
by Herbert Levine

"These poems are remarkable, radiating a love of God that is full bodied, innocent, raw, pulsating, hot, drunk. I can hardly fathom their faith but am grateful for the vistas they open. I will sit with them, and invite you to do the same."
—Merle Feld, author of *A Spiritual Life*.

What Remains
by David Curzon

"Aphoristic, ekphrastic, and precise revelations animate What Remains. In his stunning rewriting of Psalm 1 and other biblical passages, Curzon shows himself to be a fabricator, a collector, and an heir to the literature, arts, and wisdom traditions of the planet."
—Alicia Ostriker, author of *The Volcano and After*

The Shortest Skirt in Shul
by Sass Oron

"These poems exuberantly explore gender, Torah, the masks we wear, and the way our bodies (and the ways we wear them) at once threaten stable narratives, and offer the kind of liberation that saves our lives."
—Alicia Jo Rabins, author of *Divinity School*, composer of *Girls In Trouble*

Walking Triptychs
by Ilya Gutner

These are poems from when I walked about Shanghai and thought about the meaning of the Holocaust.

Book of Failed Salvation
by Julia Knobloch

"These beautiful poems express a tender longing for spiritual, physical, and emotional connection. They detail a life in movement—across distances, faith, love, and doubt."
—David Caplan, author, *Into My Garden*

Daily Blessings: Poems on Tractate Berakhot
by Hillel Broder

"Hillel Broder does not just write poetry about the Talmud; he also draws out the Talmud's poetry, finding lyricism amidst legality and re-setting the Talmud's rich images like precious gems in end-stopped lines of verse."
—Ilana Kurshan, author of *If All the Seas Were Ink*

The Red Door: A dark fairy tale told in poems
by Shawn Harris

"THE RED DOOR, like its poet author Shawn C. Harris, transcends genres and identities. It is an exploration in crossing worlds. It brings together poetry and story telling, imagery and life events, spirit and body, the real and the fantastic, Jewish past and Jewish present, to spin one tale." —Einat Wilf, author, *The War of Return*

The Missing Jew: Poems 1976-2022
by Rodger Kamenetz

"How does Rodger Kamenetz manage to have so singular a voice and at the same time precisely encapsulate the world view of an entire generation (also mine) of text-hungry American Jews born in the middle of the twentieth century?"
—Jacqueline Osherow, author, *Ultimatum from Paradise* and *My Lookalike at the Krishna Temple: Poems*

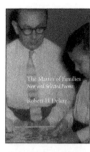

The Matter of Families
by Robert Deluty

"Robert Deluty's career-spanning collection of New and Selected poems captures the essence of his work: the power of love, joy, and connection, all tied together with the poet's glorious sense of humor. This book is Deluty's masterpiece."
—Richard M. Berlin, M.D., author of *Freud on My Couch*

There Is No Place Without You
by Maya Bernstein

"Bernstein's poems brim with energy and sound, moving the reader around a world mapped by motherhood, contemplation, religion, and the effects of illness on the body and spirit. Her language is lyrical, delicate, and poised; her lens is lucid and original."
—Anthony Anaxagorou, author of *After the Formalities*

Torah Limericks
by Rhonda Rosenheck

"Rhonda Rosenheck knows the Hebrew Bible, and she knows that it can stand up to the sometimes silly, sometimes snarky, but always insightful scholarship packed into each one of these interpretive jewels."
—Rabbi Hillel Norry

Words for a Dazzling Firmament
by Abe Mezrich

"Mezrich is a cultivated craftsman: interpretively astute, sonically deliberate, and spiritually cunning."

—Zohar Atkins, author of *Nineveh*